DUMFRIES & GALLOWAY'S LOST RA

by
Gordon Stansfield

The Stranraer Boat Express, known to all Gallovidians as 'The Paddy', at Etterby Junction Carlisle. This particular engine was a 4-4-0, no. 11, designed by J. Manson and built in Kilmarnock in 1897. It was the first four cylinder engine locomotive in use in Britain (an innovation which proved to be less economical than the old two cylinders). In 1922 the engine was rebuilt and, renamed 'Lord Glenarthur', was stationed at Ayr. It was finally withdrawn in 1934.

© Gordon Stansfield, 1998
First published in the United Kingdom, 1998,
Reprinted 2007, 2009, 2012
by Stenlake Publishing Limited
01290 551122
www.stenlake.co.uk

ISBN 9781840330571

Acknowledgements

The publishers wish to thank the following for providing the photographs in this book and additional information: Ian McDowall for pages 1, 2, 5, 6, 8, 12, 15, 26, 32, 34, 36, 38 and 41; Revd D.J. Lane for pages 3, 9, 11, 13, 18, 29 and 47; W.A.C. Smith for pages 19, 20, 23, 33, 40, 45 and the inside back cover; Malcolm Chadwick for pages 14, 16, 25, 27 and 43; Harry Jack, whose own photographs appear on page 10 and the back cover; and R. Ross Cunningham who gave permission to use his own photograph on page 46 and prints from his collection on pages 28 and 31 (these photographs were taken by H.C. Casserley and H.G. Ellis respectively).

The publishers regret that they cannot supply copies of any pictures featured in this book.

Maxwelltown, the first station west of Dumfries on the Port Road. After the withdrawal of passenger services in 1965 the line to Maxwelltown was retained for freight services to and from the ICI factory there.

INTRODUCTION

The three counties of Dumfriesshire, Wigtownshire and the Stewartry of Kirkcudbright – brought together in 1975 as the region of Dumfries and Galloway – were once well served by railways. The main services between Scotland, England and Northern Ireland all passed through the area and for the isolated counties of Galloway the railways were a boost to the local economy and a fundamental means of communication in the days before motor cars.

The first line in the area was the Caledonian Railway between Carlisle and Glasgow via Carstairs; this opened in February 1848 and became the prominent trunk route from London to Glasgow. Another route running through Dumfriesshire between Glasgow and Carlisle was the 'Nithsdale Route', opened to passenger traffic by the Glasgow & South Western Railway in May 1876. In November 1859 the Glasgow & South Western opened their line from Dumfries to Castle Douglas and in March 1861 the 53 mile extension to Stranraer was completed. The Port Road, as the route became known, was finally completed in August the following year when the branch to Portpatrick was opened.

Throughout the 1870s branch lines were built, radiating out from the Port Road to towns such as Kirkcudbright and Whithorn (which became Scotland's most southerly station) and the many villages and hamlets in between. In 1885 the line became part of the through route between London and Stranraer (and Ireland) and in the 1920s sleeper services were introduced.

Throughout Galloway impressive viaducts were constructed to carry the line over the rugged landscape and the terrain was awkward enough to cause some odd situations. For example, a crossing loop on the single line from Castle Douglas to Stranraer was established at Lochskerrow. The nearest road was five miles away so the signalman and his family had to be transported by rail. Two short wooden platforms were built and although the station was not even listed in the public timetable until 1955, unofficial stops took place to allow anglers to fish in the nearby loch. Other locals, such as those in Gatehouse of Fleet, had to walk miles to get to the station that purported to serve their town.

Throughout the golden period between 1880 and the years up to the First World War the region's railways continued to expand. In March 1905 the Cairn Valley line opened, linking Moniaive with Dumfries, and even as late as 1918 plans were afoot to build lines from Stranraer to Drummore and Parton to Dalmellington to link with the line to Ayr. As it happened, only one new line was built in Galloway after 1918 and this was the

Cairnryan Military Railway built for use during the Second World War.

Lines were lost during these years such as the Garlieston branch which was closed in 1903, but like everywhere else, most of the cuts were made in the 1950s and '60s. Branch lines to places such as Langholm and Portpatrick, both on the furthest edges of the region (east and west respectively), have long gone but some lines still remain and in Dumfriesshire particularly there have even been some revivals.

On the two main routes still operating through the county both Gretna Green and Sanquhar were reopened after their initial closure in 1965 and in total there are six stations still open on these lines (the others are Annan, Dumfries, Kirkconnel and Lockerbie). Galloway was not so lucky – the only services still running are those on the line between Stranraer and Glasgow and, for the most part, the area has returned to relative obscurity compared with more accessible parts of the country.

Hopefully this book will remind people of the region's historic railway past and rekindle memories of those bygone days.

Class 4, 2-6-4T, no. 80117, with the 6.00 pm 'Paddy' from Dumfries at Dalbeattie, August 1964

Annan Shawhill (Shawhill Junction) – Bowness-on-Solway

Passenger service withdrawn   1 September 1921
Distance (Annan Shawhill – Solway Viaduct)   0.5 miles
Company   Caledonian Railway

This route was part of the cross-border twenty mile line which ran from Kirtlebridge Station on the Caledonian main line from Glasgow to Carlisle via Carstairs, to Kirkbride Junction on the North British line from Carlisle to Silloth. The route involved crossing the Solway Estuary. Built before the famous Scottish bridges over the Tay and the Forth, the remarkable Solway Viaduct opened in 1869 and was the longest viaduct in Europe, covering a distance of one mile, 200 yards. The viaduct was constructed by the Solway Junction Railway Company who intended it for use by trains carrying iron ore from west Cumberland to the smelters in the Scottish industrial heartland of Lanarkshire. The route was devised to avoid the bottleneck of Carlisle, but the volume of coal traffic quickly diminished due to foreign imports.

A passenger service was introduced in 1870 with four return journeys on weekdays linking Kirkbride in Cumberland with Annan where passengers could change stations for Glasgow and South Western trains to Carlisle, Dumfries and Glasgow. From Annan the line headed northwards to Kirtlebridge where connections could be made with Caledonian trains to Glasgow via Carstairs.

The Solway Viaduct suffered its first disaster in January 1881 when 45 out of 197 of its piers were damaged by ice flows. This put the line out of use for 3 years while repairs took place. Although the Caledonian Railway Company operated the line on behalf of the Solway Junction Railway Company, passenger services were sparse and by 1910 return passenger journeys amounted to just three local trips and the viaduct was subject to a 20 mph speed limit. Subsequently, the viaduct closed to passenger and freight traffic on 1 September 1921.

Responsibility for the structure passed to the London Midland and Scottish Railway Company following the Railways Act of 1921 and although not in use, the viaduct posed many problems for its owners. On Sundays thirsty pedestrians from the Scottish side made frequent journeys across the viaduct into England where the Sunday licensing hours were more liberal. To prevent this a hut was built for a guard and barriers were installed at each end as a further deterrent.

The viaduct was finally demolished between 1934 and '35 and subsequently the foundations were blown up. Even then difficulties arose as debris from these damaged local fishing boats and nets, and eventually some of the larger foundations had to be broken up by hand.

Annan Shawhill (Shawhill Junction) – Kirtlebridge (Kirtlebridge Junction)

Passenger service withdrawn   27 April 1931   *Station closed*   *Date*

Distance   5.25 miles   Annan Shawhill   27 April 1931

Company   Caledonian Railway

Caledonian Railway locomotive 114, no. 14462 – the last passenger train to Kirtlebridge from Annan, Annan Shawhill Station, April 1931.

This line was the remaining section of the cross-border route to Bowness. Trains took about fifteen minutes to cover the five and a half miles and there were, on average, four return journeys Monday to Saturday and connections were available at Kirtlebridge with the Caledonian's main Glasgow – Carlisle line, and at Annan with the Glasgow & South Western's Glasgow – Carlisle line. Due to the lack of manpower caused by the war, the service, like many others on minor lines, was suspended from January 1917 to March 1919. In June 1924 the Caledonian station became known as Annan Shawhill in order to avoid confusion with the Glasgow & South Western's Annan Station. Freight services from Annan Shawhill lasted until February 1955.

Cairnryan (Cairn Point) – Stranraer (Cairnryan Junction)

Passenger service withdrawn	1945	*Station closed*	*Date*
Distance	7.25 miles	Cairn Point	1945
Company	War Department		

Known as the Cairnryan Military Railway, this line was constructed between January 1941 and July 1943. Cairnryan Junction, about a mile from Stranraer, was on the Glasgow & South Western line from Stranraer Harbour to Glasgow. For most of its route the line followed the shore of Loch Ryan, continuing to a terminus at Cairn Point which was about a mile north of Cairnryan. No stations with platforms were provided and trains stopped at suitable locations along the route as required. There were various wharves along the lochside and as the whole area was operated by military personnel a passenger service was provided between Cairn Point and Stranraer with the latter's stop at London Road Bridge. The War Department gave up the port in 1950 and subsequently the rail line and some of the port equipment were dismantled. The junction and signal box at Cairnryan Junction were closed in 1962.

The staff and Station Master with his wife and daughter, Lochmaben Station, 1904. (see opposite page).

Dumfries (Caledonian and Glasgow & South Western Junction) – Lockerbie (Lockerbie Junction)

Passenger service withdrawn	19 May 1952	*Stations closed*	*Date*
Distance	14.75 miles	Locharbriggs	19 May 1952
Company	Caledonian Railway	Amisfield	19 May 1952
		Shieldhill	19 May 1952
		Lochmaben	19 May 1952

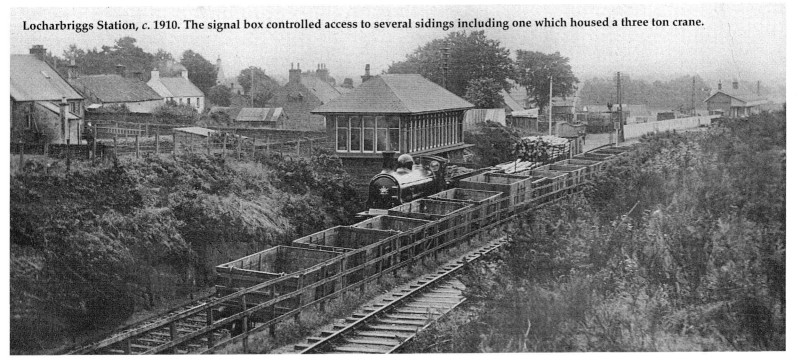

Locharbriggs Station, *c.* 1910. The signal box controlled access to several sidings including one which housed a three ton crane.

The two main lines between Glasgow and Carlisle – the Caledonian's Glasgow Central via Carstairs, and the Glasgow & South Western's Glasgow St Enoch via Kilmarnock – were linked between Dumfries and Lockerbie on 1 September 1863. The Dumfries, Lochmaben and Lockerbie Railway Company built the line but this company was owned by the Caledonian and the line was part of their scheme to create inroads into the Glasgow & South Western's territory, as well as trying to obtain a share of the Irish traffic which used the Dumfries – Stranraer route partly owned by the Portpatrick and Wigtownshire Joint Railway Company. There were about five return passenger workings over the line with trains stopping at all stations right up until closure. Connections with trains on the main lines could be made at Dumfries and Lockerbie. Freight services lasted until April 1966 although railway specials traversed the line a few times in the early 1960s.

Dunragit (Challoch Junction) – Dumfries (Castle Douglas Branch Junction)

Passenger service withdrawn	14 June 1965	*Stations closed*	*Date*
Distance	66 miles	New Galloway	14 June 1965
Compan	Portpatrick & Wigtownshire Joint Railway	Parton	14 June 1965
		Crossmichael	14 June 1965
Stations closed	*Date*	Castle Douglas	14 June 1965
Glenluce	14 June 1965	Buittle	1 October 1894
Kirkcowan	14 June 1965	Dalbeattie	14 June 1965
Newton Stewart	14 June 1965	Southwick **	3 May 1965
Palnure	7 May 1951	Kirkgunzeon	2 January 1950
Creetown	14 June 1965	Killywhan	3 August 1959
Gatehouse of Fleet *	14 June 1965	Lochanhead	25 September 1939
Lochskerrow	9 September 1963	Maxwelltown	1 March 1939

* Closed between 5 December 1949 and 20 May 1950.

** Closed between 25 September 1939 and 3 February 1941.

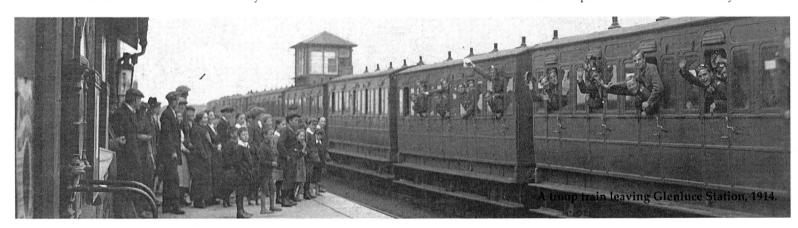

A troop train leaving Glenluce Station, 1914.

The Portpatrick & Wigtownshire Joint Railway Company was owned by a combination of four railway companies – the Caledonian, the Glasgow & South Western, the London & North Western and the Midland. The Portpatrick and Wigtownshire ran the line from Stranraer to Castle Douglas, while the last stretch from there to Dumfries came under the ownership of the Glasgow & South Western. There were two branch lines: at Newton Stewart a line ran to Garlieston (passenger service withdrawn 1903) and Whithorn (passenger service withdrawn 1950) while at Castle Douglas there was a branch line to Kirkcudbright which lasted until May 1965. The railway prospered fairly well, carrying passengers bound for Ireland as well as a large number of tourists. During the Second World War, the London Midland and Scottish was in control and a large amount of military traffic was carried, mainly in connection with secret work on a port on Loch Ryan which would have been used in the event of the shipyards on the Clyde being put out of action. The last passenger train on the line ran on 12 June 1965 and was the overnight 'Paddy' to London. Steam-hauled to the last, local residents turned out in force to wave goodbye to this once famous cross-country line.

Class 4, 2-6-4T, no. 80119, at Creetown with the 3.50 pm from Stranraer to Dumfries, August 1964.

Gatehouse of Fleet Station, April 1965. The rarity of passengers is apparent and closure was just a couple of months away.

Standard Class 4, 2-6-0, no. 76112, passing Lochskerrow with 8.00 am Stranraer to Dumfries, October 1964. The station had a passing loop, signal box and water tower.

New Galloway Station, *c.* 1910. The village was actually six miles away and it took 45 minutes for villagers to reach the station by horse-drawn carriage.

'Black Five', 4-6-0, no. 45169, at Castle Douglas double heading
the 8.15 am service from Stranraer to Carlisle, April 1961.

Lochanhead Station, *c.* **1912. Today the station house has been converted into a dwelling.**

Garlieston – Millisle (Millisle Junction)

Passenger service withdrawn	1 March 1903	*Station closed*	*Date*
Distance	1 mile	Garlieston *	1 March 1903
Company	Portpatrick & Wigtownshire Joint Railway	* Known as Garliestown until 1909.	

A goods train approaching the crossing at Garlieston.

The original station at Garlieston was a mile away from the village itself on a line which ran from Newton Stewart to Whithorn, but when this mile long branch was opened in April 1876 the original station was renamed Millisle and a new station – Garlieston – was constructed. Initially, there were four trains each way between Garlieston and Newton Stewart with a journey time of about an hour for the sixteen mile trip. However, when the line from Millisle to Whithorn was opened in 1877 a shuttle service was run between Millisle exchange platform and Garlieston. The station at Garlieston had a single platform and the line continued for a short stretch from the station to Garlieston harbour. Although the platform was lengthened it was quite inadequate for some of the passenger trains. In August 1897 a sixteen coach train was run to accommodate 750 passengers who had returned from a day trip to the Isle of Man. After arriving at Garlieston harbour they boarded a boat train special for Newton Stewart. This type of traffic was rare and in 1903 services were withdrawn. However, the Portpatrick & Wigtownshire Company provided a subsidy in order to provide a horse-drawn bus service between Garlieston and Millisle stations. Freight services lasted until October 1964 and the line was lifted shortly afterwards.

Gretna (Dornock Depot) – Gretna (Longtown Junction)

Passenger service withdrawn	After 1918	*Stations closed*	*Date*
Distance	2.5 miles	Dornock Depot	After 1918
Company	War Department	Wylies Platform	After 1918
		Gretna Township	After 1918
		Longtown Platform (Cumberland)	After 1918

The level crossing by the school, Gretna Township.

Operated and built by the War Department, this line was provided for the vast number of workers required for the munitions factory complex at Gretna. In order to accommodate the large number of workers engaged on munitions work, a large housing complex was built within the area occupied by the factory. Due to its huge size special trains were run to transport the workers from the various factory areas to their living quarters. Special stations were built for this purpose and a passenger service was operated until after the First World War. For a short distance the rail line ran parallel with the link from the west coast main line at Gretna to the Waverley route at Longtown.

Kirkcudbright – Castle Douglas (Portpatrick Line Junction)

Passenger service withdrawn	3 May 1965	*Stations closed*	*Date*
Distance	10.25 miles	Kirkcudbright	3 May 1965
Company	Glasgow & South Western Railway	Tarff	3 May 1965
		Bridge of Dee	26 September 1949
		Castle Douglas, St Andrew Street	December 1867

A 2-6-4T shunting coaches to form the 4.51pm to Dumfries at Kirkcudbright, August 1964.

The Kirkcudbright Railway, as it was known, opened in February 1864. Initially, it was an independent railway mostly paid for by local money but within a year it came under the ownership of the Glasgow & South Western who footed the remainder of the £60,000 bill. The Kirkcudbright branch was the first branch to be built off the route from Dumfries to Stranraer and was a great boon to Kirkcudbright and the surrounding area. Train services began their journey at Castle Douglas Station on the Dumfries to Stranraer line. However, quite a number of journeys originated at Dumfries. In that year there were seven arrivals and departures on weekdays. By 1949 there were six departures from Kirkcudbright but eight arrivals, including on Saturdays a late evening train from Dumfries. The Kirkcudbright branch lost its passenger service six weeks before the passenger service was withdrawn on the Dumfries to Stranraer route in June 1965.

Class 4MT, 2-6-0, no. 76073, passing the closed station of Bridge of Dee with the 1.53 pm service from Kirkcudbright to Dumfries, July 1961. The building has been restored and converted into a house.

Langholm – Riddings (Riddings Junction)

Passenger service withdrawn	15 June 1964	*Stations closed*	*Date*
Distance	7 miles	Langholm	15 June 1964
Company	North British Railway	Gilnockie	15 June 1964
		Canonbie	15 June 1964

Class 4MT, 2-6-0, no. 43011, at Langholm with the 3.30 pm to Carlisle, April 1963.

Known as the 'Muckle Toon', Langholm was served by a branch line from the Edinburgh to Carlisle via Hawick route. Riddings Junction was just inside the English border and after leaving the Waverley route the branch line crossed the nine arched Byreburn viaduct before heading westwards to Langholm. Passenger services began in April 1864 and throughout the line's lifespan some trains ran to and from Carlisle. Freight services along the line lasted until September 1967.

Gilnockie Station.

Gilnockie c.1908, was a typical country branch line station complete with a neat garden tended by the Station Master and his children (and dog!).

Canonbie Station.

Moffat – Beattock (Moffat Branch Junction)

Passenger service withdrawn	6 December 1954	*Stations closed*	*Date*
Distance	2 miles	Moffat	6 December 1954
Company	Caledonian Railway		

An ex-Caledonian locomotive, 0-4-4T, no. 55232, awaits departure from Moffat with the 3.05 pm to Beattock on the last day of services on the branch.

The small town of Moffat was lucky enough to have a branch line service which connected at Beattock with the Caledonian's Glasgow to Carlisle main line. The branch opened in 1883 and at that time Moffat was a popular spa town. A hydro was built, attracting many visitors and a high volume of passenger traffic throughout the year. In its heyday Moffat even had its own named train to and from Glasgow – the 'Tinto Express'. Freight services were withdrawn in April 1964 along with complete closure of the line. The last passenger service was a railtour special which visited the line in March 1964.

Moniaive – Dumfries (Cairn Valley Junction)

Passenger service withdrawn	3 May 1943	*Stations closed*	*Date*
Distance	18 miles	Crossford	3 May 1943
Company	Glasgow & South Western Railway	Dunscore	3 May 1943
		Stepford	3 May 1943
Stations closed	*Date*	Newtonairds	3 May 1943
Moniaive	3 May 1943	Irongray	3 May 1943
Kirkland	3 May 1943		

Apart from the station house, Moniaive also boasted a small engine shed and one engine!

Under the Light Railway Act of 1896 a railway company could build railways in rural areas that were not subject to the same standards and conditions as other, busier, lines. One such route was the Glasgow & South Western line which ran up the Cairn Valley to the small town of Moniaive. Opened to passenger traffic on 1 March 1905, the line began at a junction at Dumfries on the Glasgow & South Western's main Glasgow to Carlisle route. The line had seven stations all serving small rural hamlets. Trains took an hour to make the eighteen mile trip with two return journeys on weekdays and an extra on Saturdays. Freight services lasted until July 1949.

Dunscore Station generally had two services each way on week days with an additional one on Saturdays. On the annual occasion of Dumfries' Rood Fair passenger traffic was particularly heavy and one year a nine-coach train was required to cater for all the passengers.

Stepford Station had very basic facilities. Passenger accommodation was just a shelter – similar to the provision at many stations today.

More elaborate facilities were provided at Newtonairds Station and it also had a passing loop and a goods yard.

Portpatrick – Stranraer Town

Passenger service withdrawn	6 February 1950	*Stations closed*		*Date*
Distance	7.5 miles	Portpatrick		6 February 1950
Company	Portpatrick & Wigtownshire Joint Railway	Colfin		6 February 1950

Class 2P, 4-4-0, no. 645, at Portpatrick with a service from Stranraer, June 1937.

Portpatrick was at one time the main port for Ireland and the railway arrived in August 1862. However, by 1874 a pier had been built at Stranraer on the sheltered waters of Loch Ryan and Portpatrick lost its position of importance. The Portpatrick & Wigtownshire company, who had constructed the line hoping that it would attain main line status, could only sit and watch as it was diminished to the level of a rural branch. In 1867 there were three through journeys to Carlisle and when the line came under the ownership of the London, Midland & Scottish Railway in 1921 Sunday excursion trains were introduced including twelve coach trains from Glasgow St Enoch. When the line lost its passenger service in 1950 it was the first closure in Galloway. Latterly, there were four return journeys in each direction with trains terminating at Stranraer Town Station. The line from Stranraer to Colfin remained open in order to serve a local creamery until 1959 but thereafter the line was lifted.

Stranraer Town – Stranraer Harbour Junction

Passenger service withdrawn	7 March 1966	*Station closed*	*Date*
Distance	0.25 miles	Stranraer Town	7 March 1966
Company	Portpatrick & Wigtownshire Joint Railway		

Stranraer Town Station, August 1964. *Left*, a DMU set forming the 4.40 pm to Glasgow; *right*: 2-6-4T, no. 80119, with the 3.50 pm to Dumfries.

Stranraer Town Station, which was known simply as Stranraer until March 1953 ('Town' was added to avoid confusion with the station at the harbour), was the terminus for trains on the Portpatrick branch line as well as those from Glasgow St Enoch and Ayr, and Dumfries and Carlisle. With the closure of the Dumfries line in June 1965 and the withdrawal of services between Ayr and Stranraer Town, all the services became concentrated on Stranraer Harbour Station.

Wanlockhead – Elvanfoot (Elvanfoot Junction)

Passenger service withdrawn	2 January 1939	*Stations closed*		*Date*
Distance	7.25 miles	Wanlockhead		2 January 1939
Company	Caledonian Railway	Leadhills (Lanarkshire)		2 January 1939

Wanlockhead Station, *c.* 1905. The Caledonian locomotive 17, 0-4-4T, no. 172, was this line's first regular locomotive. The folding-down steps on the carriages were essential on this line as both Wanlockhead and Leadhills Stations had no raised platforms.

Wanlockhead is the highest village in Scotland and the Caledonian decided to obtain its first Light Railway Order to build a branch line from Elvanfoot, on their main line between Glasgow and Carlisle, to Wanlockhead. The maximum speed on the line was only 20 mph and most trains were mixed, carrying freight and passenger coaches. Leadhills was famous for its lead mines deposits but industrial traffic dwindled when the Wanlockhead Mining Company went into liquidation in 1936. The line had four return trips daily and in 1935 the London Midland and Scottish introduced a railcar service on Sundays for ramblers. The seven mile trip took forty minutes and as the line quickly lost money it was closed in January 1939.

Whithorn – Newton Stewart (Newton Stewart Junction)

Passenger service withdrawn	25 September 1950	*Stations closed*	*Date*
Distance	19.25 miles	Millisle	25 September 1950
Company	Portpatrick & Wigtownshire Joint Railway	Sorbie	25 September 1950
		Whauphill	25 September 1950
Stations closed	*Date*	Kirkinner	25 September 1950
Whithorn	25 September 1950	Wigtown	25 September 1950
Broughton Skeog	November 1885	Mains Cross	1885
Millisle (first)	1 March 1903	Causewayend	November 1885

Whithorn Station, July 1935. The station became increasingly dilapidated as the years went on and even before closure the station house had lost its awning.

Whithorn had the distinction of being the southernmost station in Scotland and, consisting of a single platform and three sidings, it opened in July 1877. The original terminus had been at Garlieston but the emphasis changed when the last section from Millisle to Whithorn was opened with Garlieston becoming a short branch line. In the line's heyday there was a horse-drawn coach connection between Whithorn Station and the Isle of Whithorn (which was known as a tourist attraction). In the year before closure there were four journeys to Whithorn on weekdays with three departures northwards from Whithorn. Freight services lasted until 1964 and enthusiast specials visited the line in 1962.

The shed at Millisle Station, June 1936.

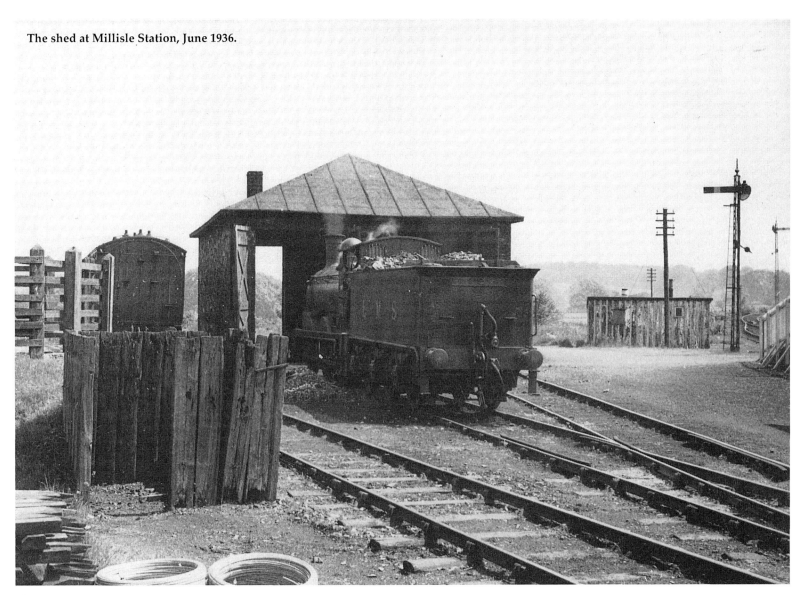

An ex-Caledonian Railway locomotive, 0-6-0, no. 57375, with an enthusiast's special at Sorbie, September 1961.

The large stone shed at Whauphill still stands, as does the Station house which has been converted into a house and post office for the nearby village.

Closed passenger stations on lines still open to passenger services

Line / Service   Gretna Junction – Glasgow via Carstairs (Caledonian Railway)

Station	Date of closure	Station	Date of closure
Kirkpatrick	13 June 1960	Dinwoodie	13 June 1960
Kirtlebridge	13 June 1960	Wamphray	13 June 1960
Ecclefechan	13 June 1960	Beattock	3 January 1972
Nethercleugh	13 June 1960		

Kirtlebridge Station c. 1904

Nethercleugh Station.

Wamphray Station. The men in bunnets are probably gangers working on the line.

The shed at Beattock Station, July 1958. *Left to right*: Locomotives 2-6-4T, no. 42214; 0-4-4T, no. 55164; and 0-4-4T, no. 55260.

Line / Service   Gretna Junction – Glasgow via Dumfries (Glasgow & South Western Railway)

Station	Date of closure	Station	Date of closure
Gretna Green *	6 December 1965	Dumfries (second)	June 1859
Rigg	1 November 1942	Holywood ***	26 September 1949
Eastriggs **	6 December 1965	Auldgirth	3 November 1952
Cummertrees	19 September 1955	Closeburn	11 September 1961
Ruthwell	6 December 1965	Thornhill	6 December 1965
Racks	6 December 1965	Carronbridge	7 December 1953
Dumfries (first)	15 October 1849	Sanquhar ****	6 December 1965

* Reopened in September 1983
** Known as Dornock until 1 May 1923.

*** Known as Kilylung until 28 October 1850.
**** Reopened in June 1994.

Gretna Green was the Glasgow & South Western's first station in Scotland.

'Black Five', 4-6-0, no. 45138, calling at Eastriggs with the 6.10 pm from Carlisle to Glasgow St Enoch, August 1964.

Ruthwell Station, 1920. A note about the station on the back of this photograph records: 'We four boys from the Manse and about 16 other pupils caught the 7.55 am train to take us to the academy – returning at 5.50 pm – between 1910 and 1925 when the local buses took over.'

Racks Station.

No. 104

AULDGIRTH

Auldgirth Station, *c.* 1918.

Thornhill Station, *c.* 1910. The station buildings remain in use today as a private residence. Like quite a few other stations, Thornhill was about a mile away from the town it served.

'Black Five', 4-6-0, no. 44718, sweeps through the old Sanquhar Station (it is now an unmanned halt) with a southbound freight, July 1963.

Station	Date of closure	Station	Date of closure
Castle Kennedy	14 June 1965	Glenwhilly **	6 September 1965
Dunragit	14 June 1965		
New Luce *	6 September 1965		

* Closed from 7 February 1882 until 16 June 1882.
** Closed from 12 April 1886 until 14 June 1886.

Castle Kennedy Station. The shed beside the house is actually an old goods wagon minus its wheels!

2-6-4T, no. 80119 at Dunragit with the 3.50 pm service from Stranraer to Dumfries, October 1964.

New Luce Station, c. 1910. Staggered platforms such as these tended to be quite rare.